Eggs, Cheese

and Butter

in

Old Regime France

Pierre Le Grand d'Aussy

Notes and translation by Jim Chevallier

Chez Jim Books

Table of Contents

About *Le Grand d'Aussy's work*

The current volume has been extracted, translated and retitled from Pierre Jean-Baptiste Le Grand d'Aussy's classic work on French food and drink, which has come down to us with the slightly misleading title of *Histoire de la vie privée des Français depuis l'origine de la nation jusqu'à nos jours*; that is, "History of the private life of the French from the origin of the nation until our days". Though Le Grand originally intended to produce such a comprehensive work, in practice he only finished the three volumes on food and drink (first published in 1783). Incomplete as these may be in terms of the overall project, they are almost manically thorough in their examination of the specific subject and have remained, over the centuries, some of the prime sources on the subject. Not only do even modern writers continue to draw on them for key information, more than one writer (in both French and English) has shamelessly copied whole stretches of Le Grand's work, well after it was written, and presented it as their own.

Le Grand at one point refers to himself as a "compiler" and certainly one of the strengths of his work is that it brings together a wealth of information drawn from earlier sources, some classics of their respective periods, some profoundly obscure. He began as a Jesuit and brings to his task the methodical, erudite and demanding precision which made the Jesuits so admired as teachers. But his personality – passionate, determined, unsparing, but also compassionate, even witty and sensual – shines through. When he thinks a previous writer has written nonsense, he says so, succinctly. When he feels obliged to work his way through fastidious, if important material, he lets his impatience show. When he includes an anecdote more because it is entertaining than because it is essential, he does so without apology. At the rare moments when he draws on his personal experience or acquaintance, he brings us vividly into the instant.

He is, in a word, not only an informative but a lively and enjoyable writer, but one who, in English, is more often cited than translated at length. The present work is part of an effort to remedy that, if only in small measure.

About this translation

Le Grand regularly includes sideheads in his text; most of the headings used here are taken from these.

This is not, in any meaningful way, an annotated edition, but some rare notes have been added here in-line, in square brackets ([]). Le Grand is also inconsistent in regard to providing dates. Since it is often helpful for the reader to know these, they have often been added here, italicized and in square brackets. A similar issue exists with Latin, which he sometimes paraphrases or even translates fully and sometimes leaves in the original; in the latter cases, a translation has been added in square brackets and quotes. The alphabetic footnotes are Le Grand's own and originally appeared at the bottom of the physical page in each case.

Both Le Grand's approach to quotes and to capitalization are inconsistent. This translation for the most part retains those of the original.

The period terms for food considered meat or meatless will be less familiar today, even in English. "Meager" for instance was once the French *maigre*, meaning "thin" but also referring to fast days or meatless foods. A meager day might also be called a "fast day" or a "fish day". "Fat" (*gras*) referred to meat or days when one could eat it; at the same time, *faire gras* ("make fat"), though it essentially meant to eat meat, also has a connotation of feasting. The French term *charnage*, though closely related to "carnage", was also used to refer to the time when meat was permitted; no true equivalent exists in English

Le Grand on Fasting, Eggs and Dairy

Le Grand titled this chapter in his larger work "Milk, Butter, Eggs and Cheese". This is already a curious title, since he never addresses milk per se in his work and the other. subjects appear in a different order in the text. But it also omits the main subject of the first section, which is that of fasting in Old Regime France. The distinction between meat (*gras*, or "fat") and meager or meatless (*maigre*, or "lean") foods was central under the French monarchy; it is referenced all through period recipe books and was enforced by law. But, as Le Grand shows, it also varied enormously over the centuries. Though, in discussing fasting and abstinence, he does indeed focus on the products listed, he also reviews the complex history of these Catholic obligations in general.

His survey here is one of the rare ones on the subject to be both concise and reasonably comprehensive. It is not complete; he omits the fact, for instance, that a Council in Orleans in 517 extended what had become largely an ecclesiastical obligation to the whole Catholic population. But the rare other works on this subject are either complete to a fault or far more cursory. (Nor is this all he himself had to say on the subject – a separate translation, *Catholic Fasting in France*, is available for readers who, in addition to this chapter, would like to read the several other lengthy passages he included on fasting.) But any reader who wants a good general introduction to this subject will find this a good one. Conversely, those whose interest is only in eggs and/or dairy will probably want to skip to those sections.

He begins by discussing the chaotic state of fasting within the Church in earlier centuries. Other historians point out that fasting had been very strict in the earliest years of the Church (often limiting people to *xerophagy*, or eating only dry foods), but as Christianity expanded to larger groups and multiple nations, the practice began to vary enormously. In particular, Eastern Orthodox practice was (and remains) stricter than that in the West.

There was also the question of whether to fast or not on specific days, like Sunday. Discussions about specifically which foods were forbidden were on-going and often local in scope. In particular eggs (and fowl in general) were sometimes viewed as acceptable, sometimes not. Butter was sometimes acceptable as a food, not (as Le Grand calls it) a "seasoning", even though dairy would later be forbidden altogether. Following a council in 817, monks without ready access to oil were allowed to use bacon fat on their food; after this was forbidden, butter became an acceptable substitute – until all dairy was forbidden in 1365. At the end of the fifteenth century, a queen's request for an exception led to its gradual return on fast days and by the seventeenth century it even seems to have been considered a standard food for fast days, as it was in Le Grand's time.

A similar process occurred with eggs, which in the centuries proceeding his had again been allowed, but only by a dispensation that was regularly renewed.

Of all this, Le Grand says, somewhat drily, "As bizarre as the opinions of men are in appearance, when one compares one century with another, they are not always as strange as they first appear. All have a principle, good or bad, on which they are based. Once you accept the principle, the result will seem correct."

Having provided this brief overview of fasting, Le Grand turns to eggs, beginning with one of what seem to be several stories about how Easter eggs came about. By his account, eggs were given special attention after Lent, when people had had to live without them. He describes celebrations – some unruly – associated with the same ceremonies which led to eggs being blessed and colored, before saying that the custom had migrated, in his time, to Russia and other countries.

He then glances at an item from Froissart which shows that egg yolks were shipped in barrels for military campaigns, before examining the ways one could preserve them (one of which sounds like a Western impression of Chinese thousand-year-eggs).

In a later section of his work, he also resumes some of the ways eggs were prepared; that section has been inserted here as well. One popular method literally resulted in... green eggs.

Le Grand begins his section on cheese with a brief look at how some special cheeses are made. (No doubt he found it unnecessary to describe basic cheese-making, since a number of works had addressed that before his own.)

The next section is on "parsleyed cheese". Already in his time this referred to blue and other cheese colored with mold, but Le Grand treats the term as if it also meant herbed cheese. This results in a passage which is one of the more confused in Le Grand's work, but which has been passed on by at least one modern writer.

Le Grand himself embellishes the original text, which is an account by one of Charlemagne's biographers of the emperor tasting a certain cheese; one modern writer not only incorporates Le Grand's version as is, but treats it as referring to a specific cheese in a specific region. For comparison's sake, here is the start of the passage from Notker the Stutterer (Balbulus), long known as "the monk of St. Gall":

> On the same voyage he arrived unexpectedly at a bishop's in a place he was obliged to pass through. As on this day he refused the flesh of quadrupeds or birds, because it was the sixth day of the week, in this place the prelate being unable to find fish on short notice, ordered that the best of cheese and of the whitest fat [*alternately*: of the best cheese, white/greasy as fat] be brought. However Charles, modest in all things and all places, to spare the prelate's embarrassment, required nothing else of him, but taking with a knife what he thought was the unappetizing rust [*sic*] and casting it aside, ate the white of the cheese. The bishop however, who was standing by like a servant, approached and asked, "Why do you do that, my lord emperor? For, what you are throwing aside is the best part." Then he, who did not know how to deceive and thought no one else would, trusted the bishop and took it and slowly ate it, and swallowed it like butter. And trying the bishop's counsel said, "True, my good host".

Note the alternate translations for the phrase *caseum et ex pinguedine canum*. Le Grand translates this plainly as "fat" (*pinguedine*) and "cheese" (*caseum*). Others have translated it in various ways suggesting that the cheese itself was white and/or greasy like fat; it is likely however that those translators were unaware that fat was not only eaten in medieval times, but was long considered appropriate for fast days.

In the original passage, the emperor is said to have so liked the cheese that he asked to be sent two carloads of it every year. The bishop, put in something of a bind, protested that he would not always know which were parsleyed or not. The emperor promptly suggested he cut each open to see and then rejoin the halves with a piece of wood. But in practice the monarch later took pity on the bishop and granted him land providing wheat and wine.

Readers conversant in Latin can read the full original passage here:

In eadem quoque profectione inopinato venit ad quendam episcopum in loco inevitabili constitutum. Cumque ipso die carnes quadrupedum aut volatilium comedere noluisset, quia sexta esset feria, pontifex ille iuxta facultatem loci ipsius, cum repente pisces invenire nequisset, optimum illi caseum et ex pinguedine canum iussit apponi. Moderatissimus autem Karolus ubique et in omnibus institutus, verecundiae praesulis parcens, nihil aliud requisivit, sed assumpto cultello, abhominabili, ut sibi videbatur, erugine proiecta, albore casei vescebatur. Episcopus autem, qui more famulorum propter astabat, proprius accedens dixit: Cur ita facis, domne imperator? Nam, quod proicis, illud optimum est. Tunc ille, qui fallere nesciret et a nullo se falli posse putasset, iuta suadelam episcopi eruginis illius partem in os proicit et sensim masticans in modum butyri degluttivit. Et episcopi consilium probans, dixit: Verum bone hospes dixisti.

Addiditque: Omnibus annis duas carradas talibus caseis plenas ad Aquasgrani mihi dirigere ne praetermittas. Ad cuius impossibilitatem rei consternatus episcopus, quasi in periculo status et ministerii sui constitutus, ei suggessit: Domine, caseos acquirere possum, sed nescio, qui eiusmodi sunt, qui vero aliter, et timeo, ne reprehensibilis inveniar apud vos. Tum io Karolus quem insueta atque incognita nequaquam fugere vel latere potuissent, dixit episcopo in talibus enutrito, et adhuc earundem rerum nescio: Incide omnes per medium, et quos tales perspexeris, acuminato ligno coniunge, et in cubam missos dirige mihi alios autem tibi et clero, vel familiae tuae reserva. Quod dum per duos annos factum fuisset, et rex talia munera dissimulanter accipi iuberet, tercio anno iam venit episcopus, et per se ipsum tanto labore et tam longe adducta repraesentare curavit. Tunc equissimus Karolus curis et laboribus eius compassus, dedit ad eundem episcopatum optimam curtem, unde frumentum et vinum ad suas et suorum necessitates ipse et successores eius habere potuissent.

Note that nowhere in this passage or beyond it does Notker give any hint as to the region where this occurred or exactly what kind of cheese Charlemagne ate. But Le Grand's version of the passage – which already confounds a blue cheese with an herbed cheese – has been read as providing one.

Le Grand then takes a glance at the cheese of Gaul – once well-known – before listing some of the more famous French cheeses of later times. A number of these – Brie, Auvergne, Franche-Comté,Roquefort, Pont-L'Eveque, – remain well-known today. A modern reader, on the other hand, may be surprised to read how many came from the Paris region or even Paris itself, just as Le Grand himself expresses surprise at reading that the cheeses of Brittany were once prized.

Of foreign cheeses, Parmesan was clearly the most prized and early on. It is not surprising that Le Grand mentions those of Holland and Switzerland as well, but somewhat more surprising today that those of Turkey came before them.

Note too that he names two different cheeses named (approximately) gruyère, one French, one foreign.

His section on dishes made with cheese is sparse, but does emphasize how often it was grilled and includes the curious fact that it was sometimes flavored with cinnamon. He also mentions two distinctive regional specialties.

His brief final section on butter starts with a survey of the best butters of his time – again, some still are known today – and ends with a look at some ways of preserving butter for transport.

Milk, butter, eggs and cheese

[FASTING]

Milk and butter, which are allowed us today, even in Lent; eggs which we only use then with a particular permission; finally cheese which we regard as a food of the most severe abstinence, have not always been, either equally allowed, nor equally forbidden. For a long time, these different substances were beyond the rules of ecclesiastical discipline; or rather the Church having not at first decided anything about which foods could be allowed or forbidden on fast days, the Faithful, for several centuries, had on that no other rule of conduct, as Doctor Launoi [*Jean de Launoi, 17th c?*] shows, than that prescribed for themselves by devotion. *Sunt & alia in catholicâ Ecclesiâ instituta vivendi præstantia*, says St. Epiphanius [*c. 315-403*]; *nimirum quod alii carnibus prorsus abstineant tam quadrupedum & avium quam piscium, nec non ovis & caseo. Alii quadrupedibus duntaxat; sed avibud ac ceteris vescuntur. Alii etiam ab avibus temperant; ova & pisces retinent; quibus nonnulli etiam abstinent, qui tamen caseum sibi permittunt. Alii verò caseo non utuntur. Præterea quidam a pane abstinent; quidam ab arborum fructibus, & coĉtis omnibus.*

"The Catholic Faithful follow, in their way of living, several commendable regimes; because some abstain not only from the flesh of quadrupeds, of birds, and of fish, but also from eggs and cheese; others give up only quadrupeds, and allow themselves birds and all other foods. Some eat no flying creatures; but they eat eggs, and fish. Others forbid themselves eggs. There are those who only use fish; there are those who, abstaining from fish, eat cheese, of which others deprive themselves. Finally, some reject bread; and others, the fruits of trees, as well as all cooked foods."

One reads the same in [*the historian*] Socrates [*born c. 380*]. *Alii omnino ab omni animantium genere abstinent. Alii inter animantia solos piscus comedunt; alii cum piscibus volucres etiam manducant, eas que ex aquâ, ut est apud Moysen, nasci asserunt...... Sunt qui cum ad horam nonam jejunaverunt, variis ciborum generibus utuntur. Aliâ ratione apud alias gentes jejunatur: cujus reu sunt cause prope infinitæ. Ac quoniam nemo de eâ re præceptum litterarum monumentis proditum potest ostendere, perspicuum est Apostolos liberam potestatem in eadem cujusque menti & arbitrio permisisse. Hanc disparem jejuniorum rationem in ecclesiis esse cognoscimus.*

"Some abstain generally from all animals; others, of all types of animals, eat only fish; others join to fish flying creatures, and think them born of water as Moses says... There are those who, when they have fasted until the ninth hour, then allow themselves various foods. Different nations have their different ways of fasting, and this diversity has an infinity of causes. Because, since no one can show in the Holy Books anything precise on this subject, it is obvious that the Apostles have left to each of the Faithful the liberty of doing in this Realm what he pleases; and that is, in my opinion, the reason for the difference in fasts which exist in the various churches."

The Historian Nikophorus says, more or less, the same thing as Socrates.

No one had, in the West, and above all in France, more set principles then in the Greek Church. Theodulf, Bishop of Orléans (797), teaching, in a lesson to the Priests of his Diocese, the foods which one may and foods which one must not allow oneself on Fast days, expressly says: *Qui ovis, caseo, piscibus, & vino abstinere potest , magna virtatis est* (a). "It is a man of great virtue who can abstain from eggs, from cheese, from fish and from wine."

Then he adds: *Vini ebrietas & luxuria prohibita sunt, non lac & ova.. Non enim ait Apostolus, nolite comedere lac & ova, sed nolite inebriari vino, in quo est luxuria.* "What is forbidden, is drunkenness and wantonness and not milk and eggs, because the Apostle does not say: abstain from eggs and milk, but he says, do not get drunk with wine which produces wantonness."

Today, we do not fast on Sundays or Lent, out of respect for this day which we regard particularly as a day of rejoicing. Then not only did one not fast on Sundays, but what is more one ate meat. A life of St. Sor [?], printed by F. Labbe in his *Bibliothèque*, proves that in the tenth c. this custom continued; since the Saint, on this day, ate stag with his own people. In certain areas, this usage continued longer still; as is seen by another life of a certain Godfrey, Bishop of Amiens towards 1100. "On the Day of Ashes [*later Ash Wednesday*], the people of Amiens having come to the church of St. Firmin, says the Legendary, the blessed Godfrey came barefoot as was his habit and covered with a haircloth to exhort his flock. He forbade them, in his speech, to eat meat from this day until Easter. But far from deferring to his orders, to the contrary they protested that they would not abandon an ancient custom; and after many complaints against their Bishop, who constantly amused himself, they said, by coming up with new austerities, they declared that they would eat meat on Sunday. They in fact did so. The Prelate knew it, but he closed his eyes , and waited for more favorable circumstances."

(a) These words of Theodulf were adopted by a Council in England, which made of them a canon.

A long time before, the Greeks had bit by bit formed, regarding the Lenten fast, a more severe moral than ours. They came to even criticize our conduct on this point. The first to adopt a rigorous stance was Photios, Patriarch of Constantinople. He offered us, on this subject, reproaches to which Ratram, Monk of Corbie, Hincmar, Archbishop of Rheims, Eudes, Bishop of Paris, and several other famous figures of the time responded. *Reprehendere moliuntur, says Hincmar in his 867 letter, quod octo hebdomadibus ante pascha a carnium, et septem hebdomdibus à casei (a) et ovarum esu, more suo, non cessamus.* ["They try to fault us because we do not abstain from eating meat eight weeks before Easter or cheese and eggs seven weeks before, as they do."]

Eudes advances, to excuse us, that Christian abstinence is a custom which varies according to the place and church. "In Italy, he says, one abstains, for three days of the week, from all food cooked with fire because this country abounds in excellent fruit of every sort. In regions which do not have available their excellent fruits, all foods are cooked by fire. In Germany, one cannot do without eggs, milk, butter and cheese; although some people deprive themselves of these voluntarily. Finally, there are people who, even on Friday and Holy Thursday, eat eggs and dairy as usual."

In regard to eggs, it is not surprising that people ate them without scruple. Opinion having established that fowl were meager [*that is, not meat*], of the same nature as fish, it was considered as a result that the egg too laid by this fowl was meager. The certificate of Charles the

---

(a) Today still the Russians, who, as is known, follow the Greek religion, abstain from butter during their different Lents.

Bald [*823 – 877*], in favor of the St. Denis Abbey, allows this Monastery, among other things, eleven hundred eggs, annually, on the three great feast-days of the year; and we know that the Benedictine Order always abstains from meat. The Abbey of St. Maur des Fosses received every year, at Ozoir, at Torcy, at Boissy-Saint-Léger, and at Ferrières, a certain number of eggs for the Monks' pittance. Finally, the Carthusians who observe a perpetual Lent and who have always observed it with the strictest regularity, ate eggs. Their rules forbid them these only during Advent; they formally allow them them during all the rest of the year.

Nonetheless, there were devout people and holy figures who were careful to avoid substances produced by animals. One reads in the life of St. Jacques, Hermit of Berry, that he *did not allow himself anything that came from flesh, such as eggs and cheese, that he only used any when he was sick; and even then one had to insist.* In that of St. Benedict of Aniane [*747 – 821*], one finds that the Saint not only forbid preparing his food with fat, (the custom has been previously mentioned, and will be again elsewhere, of Monks, who abstained from meat, seasoning their vegetables with fat); but even that he took his scruples *to the point of taking out the smallest piece of cheese.*

Besides, this rigor was only that of a few individuals. The general opinion regarded as licit what, by mortification, the latter forbid themselves; and everything, even the very praise by the Legendary of their abstinence, proves that the common people thought and acted other than they did.

It seems nonetheless that butter, either through prejudice or custom, was only eaten on fast days as a substance; and that, in kitchens, it was not at all used as a seasoning. Foods then, above all among the Monks, were prepared with oil, a custom adopted from warm countries where olive trees abound, but pastures are few; and which did not at all suit our climates, where there are many pastures and few olive trees. Thus as oil was lacking or became expensive, people were at a loss; and this inconvenience became considerable, above all for those our regions which, by their location, were far from olive regions; which is to say, for a large part of France. Complaints were made on this subject to the Council held in 817 at Aix-la-Chapelle; and the Council took notice. France having no oil, it allowed the Regular Canons to use, to prepare their food, animal fat or the oil from bacon. *Et quia oleum olivarum Franci non habent, voluerunt Episcopi ut (Canonici Regulares) oleo lardino utantur.* ["And because the Franks do not have olive oil, the Bishops want the (Regular Canons) to use bacon oil"]

Later it was found, as I have observed elsewhere, that this was a dainty ill-suited to people who had devoted themselves, as a penitence, to an austere life. The juice of bacon was forbidden; from then on it was regarded by the Faithful as meat; and so people were obliged to substitute butter for it in preparing dishes. This last substance became almost a necessity; it was combined with the most rigorous fast. This is what can be seen from a work titled *Claustro Animæ*, by Hugues de Feuillet, Abbot of St. Denis, in 1149. The author, examining what must be the food of a true Monk, says that he must live on fruits and vegetables, and that *these vegetables must be prepared, not with fat, but with butter, oil or milk*

Nonetheless, the use of butter and milk, although authorized, ended by drawing Ecclesiastic hostility. A council of Angers in 1365 condemned it, and wanted to bring back the old use of oil. *We know,* said the Council, *that in several regions not only the Regular Canons but even the Clerics use milk and butter at Lent and on fast days; even though they have fish, oil, and everything which is necessary for this period. As a result, we forbid any person whatsoever milk and butter during Lent, even in bread and vegetables; unless they have obtained a specific permission.*

As strict as was the law imposed by the Council, it was quite rigorously observed until the last years of the XVth century. The kings themselves submitted to it, as well as the rest of the Nation. Charles V, whose health was changed since he had had been poisoned by the King of Navarre, needing to ease his fast by the use of milk and butter, either as food or as seasoning, requested permission from the Holy See. The Pope, who was Gregory XI, agreed; but he demanded certificates from the Confessor and the Doctor; and even imposed on the Prince, in return, a certain number of prayers and pious works. And, showing how scrupulous people were on this sort of thing, the Pontiff in the same Bull allows the Monarch's Officers to *taste* the sauces and the stews which they make for him with butter and milk.

For lack of oil, people ate butter during Lent, as in meat-eating time [*charnaige* "carnage"], says the *journal de Paris sous Charles VI et Charles VII.*

Finally, in 1491, Queen Anne, Duchess of Brittany, had Rome solicited, as had Charles V, for permission to use butter; and, this permission, she asked, not only for herself, but for her household. The reasons she alleged to the Sovereign Pontiff was that Brittany produced no oil. Several centuries before, a similar reason had had the Regular Canons granted the use of pork. This time it earned the Queen's Household the use of butter. Encouraged by this favor, Brittany asked for and received the same favor. Our other Provinces, which had the same reason to ask it, successively requested it as well; and it is thus that we have come to enjoy it; but originally we are indebted for it to the request first presented in this matter by Queen Anne.

Nonetheless, in granting these permissions, the Holy See always added, as a preliminary and indispensable condition, that people would perform certain prayers, and above all give alms. In Paris, the Church-Wardens of Parishes asked that the destination of these alms be particularly set, and that it be applied to the upkeep or repair of churches. They obtained this; and from there were born those butter columns [*troncs à la beurre*], which for a long time survived in our parish churches, and which were then prudently eliminated, because having become useless, they were no longer anything but ridiculous.

Once familiarized with the use of butter as a seasoning during fast days, the French came to regard it as a food for fast days, when it was eaten as it was; and they ended up believing that one should only use it on fast days. At least this is what appears from a letter of Mme. de Sevigné (1680), in which this lady, describing a great feast given by the States of Brittany on the occasion of [*the birth of?*] the little Prince de Leon, which the States had held on the Baptismal font, expressed herself as follows: *It was all of Brittany, Messieurs the Lieutenant-Generals of Brittany, M. The Treasurer of Brittany... They would have danced the* passe-pied *of Brittany had there been dancing; and eaten the butter of Brittany, had it been a fast day.*

So long as milk was considered a meat and animal substance, cheese which is made of milk, was also prohibited on certain days; and this reasoning held weight. *They ate flesh in Lent, cheese, milk, and eggs, as in the meat-eating period,* says a work already cited above, *le journal de Paris sous Charles VI et Charles VII.* We who, since the permission granted by the Sovereign Pontiff, are used to considering butter and milk as fast-day foods, we use cheese in times of fasting and abstinence; and we reason as solidly as our Fathers, even if the result of their doctrine and of ours are opposed in contradiction. As bizarre as the opinions of men are in appearance, when one compares one century with another, they are not always as strange as they first appear. All have a principle, good or bad, on which they are based. Once you accept the principle, the result will seem correct.

When opinion had changed on the nature of flying creatures, and they were no longer considered fish, then necessarily opinion changed regarding eggs. These became like birds, a food prohibited on fast-days, or at least in Lent. The permission granted for butter emboldened people to ask that for eggs; but the latter must have been harder to obtain; because, in fact, an excellent reason existed to ask the first, the lack of oil; but what pretext could be offered for the second? Some were presented nonetheless; and Julius III, in 1555, granted the dispensation. Nonetheless the prejudices on this subject had become so strong that the Papal Bull was burned, says Sauval [7], by Order of Parlement. Despite the Bull, a Council of Bourges, in 1584, forbid using eggs in Lent unless one was sick. Soon however people felt the advantage of a favor by which everybody won; but nonetheless episcopal authority has made of this but a passing favor. The dispensation is not, like that of butter, perpetual; it must be requested every year from the bishop of the diocese; and no one is unaware that it is the occasion for a procession during the first week in Lent.

EGGS

Easter eggs

If it was difficult to abstain from eggs for forty whole days, it must also have been a great joy to return to their use when the time of penitence had just ended. Devotion, which in some periods is introduced everywhere, even made of this time a religious ceremony. One went to church, on Holy Friday and Easter, to offer eggs and have them blessed. These blessed eggs, taken back by families, gave rise to a sort of festival and rejoicing. Relatives, neighbors, friends sent them to each other; and from there came the expression *give Easter eggs*. To decorate the present, they were dyed red or blue; they were spotted, they were speckled with different colors. Finally, the gift or the sending of eggs became so general a custom, that in many cities it gave rise to a superstitious but agreeable abuse.

On one of the days of the week of Easter, the Students of schools, the Clerics of churches, the youth of the city, gathered in the public square to the sounds of rattles and drums.; these were armed with lances or sticks. From the square, they went, with the awful racket one can readily imagine, from such a crowd, at the outer door of the principle church of the place. There, they sang Laudes; after which they spread out through the city to beg for Easter eggs.

In some Provinces, the egg procession was set on the Thursday of mid-Lent. But, since one could then not ask for eggs, some other item, which nonetheless bore the same name, was received.

At Court, the custom was, on the day Easter, to take to the King's, after high mass, painted and gilded eggs. His Majesty distributed these to his Courtesans. This custom has only been abolished for thirty years { *that is, in around 1750*]. It still continues in Russia, and at the Court of several Sovereigns.

Most of our Provinces have kept that of hard-boiled and painted eggs, as presents, on the day we are speaking of. At Auxerre, they are called *roulées* ["rolleds"], because they are used as balls, for a certain game which involves reaching, by *rolling* [*rouler*] them, a certain goal.

Hard-boiled eggs used at sea

Among the provisions of food with which Sailors loaded their vessels for long trips, or for expeditions, were normally egg yolks (hard boiled eggs, no doubt). Beaten and put in barrels. Froissart [*c. 1337 – c. 1405*] counts these among those which Charles VI had embarked on his fleet, when he was contemplating an attack on England. *The vessels were filled*, he says, *with salted meats and fish, wine, cervoise* [beer], *barley, oats, rye, garlic, onion, broad beans, hay in barrels, wax candles, bottles of verjuice, bottles of vinegar, pots, mugs, wooden and tin spoons, candle holders, basins, fattened pigs, skewers, kitchen equipment, bottling equipment, salt, biscuits, flour, fat and BEATEN EGG YOLKS IN BARRELS.*

Ways of keeping eggs fresh

For a long time a way was sought to keep eggs fresh, that is, to keep them always full; because a full egg is a fresh egg; it only changes because it has let a part of its substance sweat out through its pores. To prevent this evaporation, our old books on agriculture advise putting eggs in water, in oil, in sand, in bran, in ashes, in salt, in sawdust, etc.

In Asia, they are kept, it is said, by covering them with a layer of ash moistened with sea water. Ordinary water would have this same effect; and the process, if the coating did not chap when drying, would be one of the greatest advantage, because it more completely and immediately stops up the pores.

Reaumur teaches another one, which he claims to be more convenient and faster; that is, to put mutton fat on the fire, and to dip the egg in it when it starts to melt. Such a plaster is enough, he says, to stop all loss of substance.

Finally, I have heard the Abbé Nollet, in his lessons of experimental Physics, also propose a method. "At the start of the autumn," he says, "take a certain quantity of fresh eggs, unfertilized; that is, laid by hens who will have been separated from the rooster for a month. Attach to their tips, with a little Spanish wax, the two ends of a bit of thread; this thread will then form a ring by which you will hang them from a nail. Have in a vessel, or in a large goblet, a certain amount of varnish. The best of all, because it is the cheapest and the easiest, is that which can be made with common Spanish wax, reduced to powder, and infused in wine spirits. You successively put your container under each of the eggs; you will plunge them in it; and that will be enough to preserve them. If you then want to cook them, or even set them to brood supposing they have been fertilized, you have only to rub them with a brush dipped in pure wine spirit. The varnish will disappear; and the shell will stay clean, without having its pores clogged and without that oily, disgusting appearance which results from the fat method."

[Early ways of preparing eggs]

From a later section in Le Grand's work (II: 233-234)

Eggs, which according to one of our kitchen sayings we can prepare today in a hundred and one different ways, only had twenty, in Platina's time [1421 – 1481]. Further these twenty, for the most part, differed from ours. Scrambled eggs, for example, were made with butter, water, cheese and aromatic herbs; then they were made green with the juice of borage or parsley; because this color was greatly prized in stews. Poached eggs, which our Cooks serve with a little meat gravy, and upon which they sprinkle a little pepper, were served with orange juice and sweet spices. Finally, there were still more difference for the eggs which we call today *à la trippe**, and which were then called *cut*. So many things went into them, so difficult a sauce was made, that they only resemble ours in being hard and chopped into pieces.

---

* Hard-boiled eggs cut into rounds and browned in butter with parsley, salt and pepper, then lightly boiled with sweet cream. "Trippe" might be derived from "trique-madame", also "orpin blanc", or white stonecrop. [JC]

CHEESE

Making cheese

It is likely that the general procedures for making cheese have always been the same; but the respective situations of each of the different regions of France must nonetheless have introduced local differences in the process. "In Auvergne," says Champier [*1560*], "Cheese was highly salted; elsewhere it was salted little; in the Autunais, it was not salted at all, because salt was too expensive there."

According to de Serres [*1539 – 1619*], to form an excellent cheese, it had to be made with cow's milk, goat's milk and sheep's milk, mixed together. "Each of these different milks," he says, "will give it good qualities; as the old proverb has it, *cow's butter, sheep's cheese, goat's curds.*"

This author also wanted that one practice in France the procedure used at Lodi and at Parma to make these cheese known *to everybody for their goodness.* "One sees," he says, "that in some parts of Switzerland, people try to imitate Parmesan"; but, he complains that the French neglect it, except in certain regions.

Parsleyed cheese

[Note: by Legrand's time, the French phrase fromage persillé *already referred to veined cheeses like blue cheese, whose veins (when green) were sometimes thought to look as if made with parsley. But today those are created using bits of bread, not herbs, and Le Grand's account seems to confuse herbed cheeses and cheese treated to produce veins. Note too that he distorts the quoted text.]*

For a long time people have known the art of parsleying cheese; that is, of putting in the curds when making it, certain herbs which, in imparting to it their taste (a), further give it veins or green stains, rather agreeable to the eye. This second is at least nine centuries old, as proves the following anecdote about Charlemagne, reported by the Monk of St. Gall.

"The Emperor during one of his trips," says the Historian, "arrived suddenly and unexpectedly at a Bishop's. It was a Friday, The Prelate had no fish; and he did not dare, because of the day's abstinence, serve the Prince meat. He gave him then what he had at his place, fat and cheese. Charles ate the cheese, but, taking the parsleyed stains for mold, he was careful beforehand to remove them with the tip of his knife. The Bishop, who was standing by the table, as well as the Prince's retinue, took the liberty of telling him that what he was throwing away was the best part of the cheese. And so Charles tasted the parsleyed part; he found that his host was right, and even commanded him to send him, every year, at Aix-La-Chapelle, two cases of such cheese. The latter answered that it was well within his power to send him cheese, but not to send it parsleyed, because it was only in opening it that one could be sure the merchant had not made a mistake. Well then, said the emperor, before sending them off, cut them down the middle; it will be easy to see if they are as I wish then. You will have only to attach the two halves, in joining them with a wooden pin; then you will put everything in the case."

(a) The Romans mixed thyme, reduced to powder, in theirs. Still today, certain regions of Lorraine make cheese in the curds of which they sprinkle fennel seeds.

Gallic cheese

Our different Provinces have always each had cheeses which were more or less prized; there are even few countries which can boast of having so many, and so many good ones, as France. Pliny states that, in his time, those of Nimes, as well as those of Mont Losère in the Gevaudun and neighboring areas were sought in Rome; but these cheeses, says the Naturalist, had the inconvenience of not keeping; one had to eat them fresh.

Martial mentions those of Toulouse.

The most famous French cheeses

Under the Kings of the third race [*that is, the Capetians*], Chaillot, a village near Paris, made some that were sought in the Capital. The inhabitants even had the right to send their cows to graze on that island in the Seine which used to be called Mackerel and which now is called the *Isle des Cygnes* [*the Island of Swans*]; but in return, they were obliged to present, every year, to the St. Germain Abbey, on the day of the Ascension, two large bouquets, six small, a parisis denier for each cow, and a fat cheese.

In the XIIth and XIIIth centuries, those of Champagne, and above all of Brie, were prized.

This last, which is still singularly prized today, is named several times with praise by our Fabulists and our old Poets. It was cried in the streets; but Eustache Deschamps [*1346-1406*], a Poet who wrote under Charles VI, says archly that it was the only good thing which came to us from Brie. Today we have two sorts of these: table cheeses and those which, being liquid, arrive in pots. These last are known as Meaux cheeses. In the class of the first the best are those of Nangis.

By the statues given to the Pastry-makers in 1522, the King allowed these artisans the right to inspect the Brie cheese sold in Paris and its suburbs; *given that these Pastry-makers have an interest in this, since they daily use the said merchandise.*

Platina (1509) cites among the good cheeses those of Chaunay in Picardy, of Bréhémont in Touraine, of the grande Chartreuse in the Dauphiné, of the Epine and of Rosanais in Burgundy.

Charles Etienne praises those of Craponne in Auvergne, those of Béthune in Flanders, the *Angelots* of Normandy, and the fresh cream cheese which Montreuil and Vincennes supplied to Paris.

Champier, who speaks with praise of these last, says that the peasant women brought them to town in little rush baskets, and that they were eaten sprinkled with sugar. Today, not only Vincennes and Montreuil but almost all the villages near the Capital daily send some like them. The most esteemed are those of Viri. The Abbé of Marolles, in the last century, said that Parisians sought out also those of Vannes, Clamart, Monteruil and Grobois (a).

The same Champier also praises those of the Chartreuse, of Bréhémont, of Bethune, and of Craponne; which, all four, have already been cited. He says of the *Angelots* that they are agreeable, but that

(a) This testimony of the Abbé de Marolles is found in the translation he published of Martial in 1635. Regarding what the Latin poet says about the cheeses of Toulouse, his translator gives us, in a note, a very long list of all the cheeses of France which had some reputation.

they do not last. In the list, he adds the *rougerats* of Lyon, the cheeses of Brienne, of Bresse, of Sens and of Limoges. But he puts above all those of Auvergne, the round as well as the cylindrical ones, and even regards these two types as the best in Europe.

According to Liébaut [*1535-1596*], the people of Auvergne used the most meticulous and the most careful cleanliness in making their cheeses. They took their care, he says, to the point of only using children of fourteen, very neat and very healthy.

The same author speaks of cheese for Lent called *à la chardonette [that is, with thistle down]*, and curdled with pike eggs and of certain other small cheeses which in Paris were called *jonchées*, and which were made of cheese curdled without any pressure.

Chasseneux [*Barthélemy de Chasseneuz, 1480-1541*], in his *Catalogus Gloria Mundi* [*1540*] (a), counts among the excellent ones those of Brie, of Entigny near Dijon, and those which were called in Bresse, because of their round shape, *death's heads*, or *Monk's heads*.

De Serres praises the *little fromageons* of Baux in Provence, the angelots of Brie, and *above all* the cheeses of Brittany. De Serres' use of this term *above all* is all the more surprising in that Brittany is not named by any of the Authors cited above, and even today its cheese has no reputation. This is no doubt an error on the part of the Writer.Nonetheless, on the other hand, since from time to time tastes change, a passing caprice might have given those of which we are speaking a moment of favor. This favor, further, if it ever existed, did not last long.

(a) What regards cheese in the *Catalogus* of Chasseneux is taken from another work, on this subject, by a certain Pantaléon de Conflans.

The Abbé of Marolles, in the list which he has left of the most famous cheeses of France, has no praise for those of Brittany. He had a modest opinion of those in Poitou, and a low one of those of Anjou and the Limousin. The best, according to him, were the cream cheeses of Blois, and those from around Paris, already cited above; these were the angelots; these were the *hearts* of Gournay and of the country of Brie, of Linas, of Roche, of Roquefort (a), of Berny, of Beauvais, of Peyrnez, of Fleurs, of Couzieres, of Traye, of Boisjency, of Aunay, of St. Laurent-des-Eaux, of Vauduloir, of Montmaraut, of Traversay, Livarot, Pont-L'Eveque, Marolles and St. Eure-de-Toul.

In certain parts of the mountains of Franche-Comté, named Gruyères, cheeses were made, at the end of the last century, which bore the same name. The Memoir of the Intendant of this Province (one of those which the different Intendants of the Kingdom provided in 1698, by order of the King, to the Duke of Burgundy for the instruction of this Prince) informs us that *these cheeses were sold all over France, and that peasants gained considerably, during the war by carrying them themselves in the armies of Italy and Germany.*

(a) This became one of the best and the most esteemed in France. M. Marcorelle, who has published a curious memoir on this subject, informs us that annually six thousand quintals [*1 quintal=100 old pounds, c.48,951 kg*] come from the cellars of Roquefort, without counting twelve hundred quintals, which several neighboring villages sell under the same name.

Foreign cheeses

The cheeses of Italy were introduced late into the Kingdom. Parmesan, so prized today, was only known there under Charles VIII [*1470 – 1498*]; it was only, if one is to believe André de la Vigne [*c. 1457-c. 1527*], by a sort of luck. When the Monarch, in his Naples expedition, passed through Piacenza [*Plaisance*], says the Historian, the Townsfolk came to offer him several cheeses. But he was so struck by their enormous size (the Chronicle following Monstrele describes them as *almost as large as millstones*), that, out of curiosity, he sent one of them to the Queen and to the Duke of Burgundy., who was then in the Bourbonnais. The Count found it excellent, and people so got a taste for it that in the following century, according to Champier, it was that which was the best regarded.

The same author informs us that the most esteemed of foreign cheeses, after Parmesan, was that of Florence called *Marsolin*. This one, he says, was shaped like a cucumber.

De Serre (1600) again assigns the first rank to Parmesan, which he calls a cheese of Milan or of Lombardy, and which he too describes as being as big as a millstone. He gives the second to the cheese of Turkey, which came to us in bladders; the third to that of Switzerland, and the fourth to those of Holland and of Zealand; "countries," he says, "so abundant in pastures, that a cow there gives thirty [*French*] pints of milk and sometimes as many as forty; countries, finally, which, despite their lack of breadth, produce as much milk in a year as all of la Guyenne, in the same time, produces wines."

Gontier (*de Sanitate tuendâ*, 1668), names among the excellent foreign cheeses that of Gryeres [*sic*].

Cheese dishes

It has been with the taste for cheese as with that for pâtés. We regard them today, the one as the other, as suited only to Germany, England and Italy; and for a long time the one or the other was the delight of our Fathers. Though an old proverb declares:

> No wise man
> Ever ate cheese.

although a similar *saying* is cited from the Cardinal de Peronne [*1556-1618*], *stingy hand, good cheese*; it was nonetheless used in an infinity of dishes; it was included in a variety of pastries. There were even some sorts which were eaten grilled. The Roman de Clais, a manuscript, speaking of a town under assault, says

> Many good barrels of wine are found,
> Much good pork, much cheese to grill

This cheese was cut in slices; these slices were put on the grill or in the frying pan; and they were then sprinkled with sugar and cinnamon. Platina writes that that of Auvergne above all was excellent grilled.

Often, instead of grilling the cheese, it was melted on the fire in an iron utensil, hollow and especially made; then it was poured this way on a piece of toast, burning, that was seasoned in the same way with cinnamon, sugar and other spices. It was particularly in his way, according to the same author, that those of Bresse were eaten; and, according to Champier, those of Craponne.

Sérat

The Normans had a way using their milk which was particular to this Province. They boiled it with garlic and onion. This soured liquor they called *Sérat*, say Champier and Liébaut, and they kept it, for their use, in particular vessels.

Brousse

In Provence, according to Gontier, another dish was known of the same sort called *brousse*, but more appetizing. It was milk which was heated on a low fire so that, without boiling, it could nonetheless foam and rise. This sort of foam was successively skimmed with a spoon and it was served at the table, sprinkled with sugar.

BUTTER

The most esteemed butters

Champier reports that Blois and Lyon greatly esteemed their butter. In Paris, he says, the most sought for the table is that of Vanvres [*today, Vanves*]. Charles Etienne says the same thing of this last. In the last century, Sauval regarded it as the *best butter in the world*. It still enjoys today a great reputation; however preferred to it is the butter of l'Enfant-Jesus, so named for a religious Community established in one of the suburbs of the Capital, where it is made (a).

Mme de Sevigné praises that of la Prévalaye near Rennes. *We make innumerable buttered breads of them*, she says in one of her letters. *We put in them small fines herbes and violets.*

When Louis XIV had given the Menagerie of the Trianon to the Duchess of Burgundy, this Princess, says Mme du Noyer in her letters, got such a taste for it, that she *went herself to milk the cows, and she made butter there which was served on the King's table, which His Majesty found admirable, and which one was obliged to eat to pay him court.*

The Nation which consumes the most butter," adds Champier, "Is the Flemish. Not a day, not a meal gone by without eating it and I am surprised it has not yet tried to put it in its drink. And so in France it is called, in derision, "the butter maid", and when someone must travel in that country, it recommended that he take a knife, if he wants to try good lumps of butter."

a. This Community, established in imitation of that of St. Cyr, to raise thirty -three poor maidens, owes its origin o the late M. Languet, the parish priest of St. Sulplice, founder of several other very admirable establishments.

"The French," the author continues "nonetheless and above all in the month of May, serve fresh butter on their tables. As to the common people, they eat it in the morning with garlic in order to drive out what they call bad air and kill any worms they might have in their guts."

By the craft with which we make butter, we know how to keep it fresh, at least for a few days. It is something we have come to by what is called after Gournay. Merchants from French Véxin go to this small town; they re-knead it in water, work it again, wash it to purge it of any milk and serosities it might still contain and which soon would spoil it. Then they put it in large slabs of from forty to sixty pounds and send it to Paris where it is used in kitchens.

Salted butter

Brittany and Normandy, Provinces long known for their butter, had conceived of another way of preserving it, by salting it, more or less like meat; something which was all the easier for them since, by their position along the Ocean, they could acquire salt at low cost. Thus seasoned, they put these in a long cylindrical earthen pot and sent it everywhere in the Kingdom.

Champier informs us that, in his time (1560), these two Provinces used this method; but it is older than him; the Statutes given in 1411 to the Paris Fruitsellers speak of *salted butter in earthen pots*.

Charles Etienne [1504–1564], discussing salted butters, and in particular for the kitchen, puts in first place that of the Ile de France; in second, that of Normandy, in third, those of Flanders and Brittany.

Melted butter

To preserve butter, there was another process, which was to melt it; which, says de Serres, *makes it finer.* "While it is on the fire, it is skimmed," he adds. "After which, when it has become clear and blond like fine olive oil, it is poured into large varnished earthen vessels." This was, according to the author, the method *used in Lorraine,* which proves the rest of France was unaware of it still; and that it is to this Province that we owe it."

THE END

www.ingramcontent.com/pod-product-compliance
Lightning Source LLC
Chambersburg PA
CBHW070236290526
45789CB00004B/1651